NOTES TOWARDS AN ESCAPE FROM DEATH

NOTES TOWARDS
AN ESCAPE FROM DEATH

by

Dionyse McTair

NEW BEACON BOOKS
London   Port of Spain

First published 1987
by New Beacon Books Ltd.,
76 Stroud Green Road, London N4 3EN, England

© 1987 Dionyse McTair

All rights reserved. No part of this book may be reproduced in any form or by any means without prior written permission of the publisher, excepting brief quotes used in connection with reviews written specifically for inclusion in a magazine or newspaper

ISBN 0901241776 hardback
     0901241784 paperback

Printed by Villiers Publications Ltd
26a Shepherds Hill, London N6 5AH, England

Contents

Song	9
For A Friend	10
Dance	11
Surrender	12
Poem For Pat	13
It Is Not Yet The Evening Of Our Days	14
'If you love somebody . . .'	17
Looking At You Across The Room	18
Question	19
Answer?	20
Waiting	22
Morningstar	23
For Isioma — Asleep	24
The Longer Road Beyond	25
Afterglow?	26
The Cricket Sings	27
Solidarity	28
It Could Only Be	30
The Tender Web	32
Dialogue	35
'death stalks . . .'	36
'Silence bears the colours . . .'	37
Workers In His Vineyard	38
Conference Jan. '71	39
Learning	40
Dip. Ed. 1984	41
Grenada Oct. 19 1983 (for the Caribbean)	42
The Gathering (T&T 12.8.86)	45
To My Butterfly	46
Rebirth	47
'Cinders ebb . . .'	48

Dance II	49
Dawn: Mist Over Santa Cruz	50
The Visit	51
Silent Shades	52
'roots stalk fluid earth . . .'	55
'a tattered flame . . .'	55
'wings pierce . . .'	56
'a tremulous wave . . .'	56
'gentle reeds . . .'	57
'victory spawns tentacles . . .'	57
'incandescent waters . . .'	58
'battered sinews . . .'	58
'darkness throttles blinding night. . . .'	59
Notes Towards An Escape From Death	63

ACKNOWLEDGEMENTS

Conference Jan. '71 First published in *The Shape of Things to Come*, Scope University Press, U.W.I., Mona (1971); subsequently published in *Caribbean Quarterly*, vol. 18, no. 4, December 1972.
Solidarity Published in *Experiment 1*, The Literary Society, Creative Arts Centre, U.W.I., Mona (1972).
Home Published in *Kalaloo*, The University Literary Society, Creative Arts Centre, U.W.I., Mona, May 1973.
The Cricket Sings Published in *Kalaloo*, The University Literary Society, Creative Arts Centre, U.W.I., Mona, May 1973.

DEDICATION

for Gabre, "... a wonder-
ful
of joy
of loveliness"
and for Pat.

a
   child
is
   a
   flower

Song

Among the dewy fresh silence of mountain paths
embroidered with shadows
of shimmering gold
I wander this flaccid moon

Lost in this maze
perched upon a twig of rain
I sing out my lonely earthly twitter
my cheeping chirping plea
for life

Borne of this tempest
the placid sun
lives
      conceived in pain
dies
      consumed in silence
and I wait again
another dawn
for one to hear
for one to care for
                        this is my song
                        my prayer at evening

For a Friend

Now the adolescent tears are falling
there is no need to dry them off.

A lifeless stream off course
trusts waterfalls of wonders
cascades into dunes — my temple.

In the silence of growing things
we cast a tireless dirge
and resurrect the primeval essences.

Dance

Fingers wean from timeless ripples
night's faun quivering through the sand
eyes reel mourning incense

o my tired sage. . . .

SURRENDER

Flowers pierce an open heart
soaring in a gleaming sea
of tears
and yet, sometimes
an old heart
chimes
a new song. . . .

Poem for Pat

Shades and shadows abound around you
Trinkets form a dismal chain

Gnawing at dimness to reveal a vision
Ripe with torment
tinkling through pain. . . .

It is Not Yet the Evening of Our Days

Wings fold and clasp
yielding sparkles
dewdrops of night

children twitter
lantern beacons
twilight maims a falling shadow

retreat in quiet rumination
echo the manic symbolism of time
drench the twitching cartilage asunder

twice beguiled
the token manifolds of light
quench a thirsting rage for cues extant

live in tune
sweetly murmuring and unsung
wrench seaming shoals away from shallow moorings
and claim the day with terror and delight.

*I saw my soul
through a crack in your heart
and we shall never be the same again.*

If you love somebody
it shouldn't make you
cry

Looking at You Across the Room

Eyes hatch a mellow smile
fade into a vision of chilly streams
where words dance in the seaborne wind

and I cry out. . . .

Question

Is it what I need
or what I want
that comes along?

a-
light
a-
blaze
burning mad
mid-
day sun
warping
twisting
bending
me
in its fury
head-
on
head-
down
I writhe
worm-like
to face it.

ANSWER?

How can I say
I love you
when each time
I search your
eyes
I see
again
the uncertainty
the pain?
How can you truly
care
when time and
I
fleeting poui petals
you have made to
blossom
drop by
and out
again?
And even if
we were to stay
would you again and
again
make me understand
that people are for
real
that love, though
silent
can be
true?
would you, over and
over
let me cling to
you

from the cold
outside
make me want
to always
feel
your simple desires
and with you, realise
them?
Will I ever be
close to
you
And am I
now?

Then,
if by chance
you answer
yes
to all these things
will I still be
afraid
and run away
with the
dawn?

Waiting

Must you always go
and stay only in dreams?

Your words still fall
soft —
dewdrops on dawning sands
a mother's hands
in weaning.

If only you could come to me
now
in dreams, my only reality
I could expand, vibrate
echo of rhythms loud and true
step out of the encampment
that is my soul.

Then together we'll walk
the frothing
foam-filled shore
that builds my castle.

To touch an ear
or even a heart
is always.

Morningstar

Do not accuse me, morningstar
who await the fragrance
of dawn's mantle
to wade the waters
of life's torrential rivers,
plunging reflections of absence,
till the swishing tide of morning
blows its ephemeral bubbles
and spews us once again
on to the chugging distances
of an endless day.

Stay then, morningstar
twinkle my nun's dream
into ashes
cast it at my feet,
garlands of decaying imagery,
wisps of light
glow into the haunting scent
of molten night.

For Isioma – asleep

Slipping into innocent oblivion
what dreams do a child dream?
your dream — world
your whole world
my world
must be a wonder-
ful
of joy
of loveliness.
But is there too the pain
of waiting
of knowing
that with new moons
you grow towards
a cherished womanhood
of sighs
of solitude?

The Longer Road Beyond

The wind
whistling through your graceful branches
rustles your leaves
and soothes my tortured soul.

You bathe me in your golden splendour
that trickles down
wavering with the wind
and I grasp wildly
for one last ray of hope.

Why do you flutter away
carrying in your feather-like
wake,
my dream?
Why must you take the longer road
beyond this quiet river?

Yes,
you always crave the turbulent ocean
that tosses my crumpled body
through her savage waters
until she vomits me
upon another shore
renewed, restored
and strengthened
in my tireless quest.

Afterglow?

But your scent remains with me
here, on the pillow
and the milk of our desire
mingles with my tears
and curdles
at the image of cells
fondling inside me
fumbling,
        searching,
stretching me
        kicking at my walls
enlarging my world
  bigger
      and bigger
          and bigger
bringing into my life
a priceless joy —
because of you.

The Cricket Sings

And the cricket sings
this night
for me
heralding the rain
to suckle this arid land.
A soft fragrance
floats gently upwards
paying homage to the sky
for its blessing
and all is fresh again
except my soul
that will not be comforted
by the cricket's croaking chorus
or by the sky, crying its silent sorrows
on to a land
that issues from the tomb
of her ravaged womb
the fetid stench of carrion
through the air
    .... you have quenched my thirst
    but what of my hunger?

Solidarity

Alone again
fleeing through dense clouds
cushioned by thoughts
of you
with me
somewhere
always around
but mostly
inside
filling me
with you
yourself
your spring-fresh beauty
dimpled inundations
of understanding
seeping through
warm-brown eyes
finger-tip gentle
on a harrowed soul.

Is it this once
that untold reality
that brings me here
somewhere
with you
around me
over me
in me
throbbing
searching
rampaging
through your world
piercing
nakedly and unashamedly

finding in you
that me I dare
this once
to give and share?

But where can we
be truly free
to explore and create
unhindered by needs and notions
spirits rebellious
against systems and obligations
that choke and rob?
How can we make
of this short dream
a totally fulfilling reality?

Maybe someday
we'll find our world
ensconced
somewhere
in river valleys
a stone's throw from reality
beneath cocoa trees
nurtured in bronze earth
moist and fertile
streaking sunlight
through shading leaves.

It Could Only Be

It could only be
because
I know your
agony
your pain.
It could only be
because
I see you
hanging
by
the fleeting
tether of
life
fleeing the soft
caresses of
evening
for the
still-born
echoes of
night,
jostling shadows,
death
gnawing on
a gentle
soul.
It could only be
because
you know that
immortal
moment
within the purple blush of dawn
where tender
tide
embraces

night
and
day —
and anxiously
turn
away.
It could only be
because
I hear you
pleading
softly above
the tin-pan
din of
day
to be
let
in —
   a lone wanderer
   yet homeward bound —
It could only be
because I
love
you.

The Tender Web

You seep within the limits of my need
and weave me in a tender web of care

Taut among these moving shackles
a wisp of shadowy faith appears

*It is
difficult
to find
a black cat
among the
shadows*

DIALOGUE

Cobwebs tear
at these grey etchings.
Passion twitches into myopic frenzy
grown flaccid
with platitudes.

death stalks
the avid hunter
and dark illusion
fades softly
by

Silence bears the colours
of death
and sadness mocks
the cold dark treachery
in time

Workers In His Vineyard

And in your mocking goodness
a shred of charity remains.
Blazing errant trails of Grace
your tainted gifts lie lame
as vaunted shadows

.... a Ghost so Holy he remains
the one redeeming act
of Grace.

Conference Jan. '71

We watched our own blood die
Mocked images in mirrors
Spat.

Will not the echoes of silences
rippling through wind-blown lakes
bind us as shadows to their source?
Will ever the void of voices
chant not chatter
of words that fall
drooping thick-red curtains
on thread-thin ears?
Will always the offering
in honour of the people
stink of scholarship and rhetoric?

To live within the moment is the message.

Fingers on hilltops
lick sticks of grass and mud.
Asses graze on sand.

LEARNING

Step up and walk
these learned steps
to knowledge.

To live is to reach
beyond this scramble.
To reach is to make
the break that bends
the mind
towards this unreality.

To reach
to make
to break
then bend
away
from this waste
from these chaste-
ned chastised
brains
is not to talk
in tongues
heavy laden with
the crumbs and crusts
of a civilization
that grovels in pits
of war and hate
to give us
of its learning.

Dip. Ed. 1984

jettisoned by.

you whisk unimpeded through minds of hay
great orator,
lend us your ear but not your heart

brief flight
solemn machinations

back to earth in a flash of fantasy
flown into reality

GRENADA OCT. 19 1983
(for the Caribbean)

Catch a spell
bound in dust
reeking of master, mongrel, hatchet
men steeped and divided
necessary to tramp and romp
home is still a place of sorrow

*Home is
peace
and God
is not
tall.*

The Gathering
(T&T 12.8.86)

Minstrels of the universe
daubed in light
chart the fog infested waters

Children of the truth
scampering headlong into eternity
peel ribbons of slime
off mankind's sacred dross

Heeders of the call
singular in nature
before the helm
a tortuous gaze must rest

To My Butterfly

As we sail along
lotus-like
two silver ponds
in a sea of darkness,
we touch
and flow into each other's
stillness
to become one teardrop
of God

Rebirth

And you
with tender radiance
accept the seed with awe.

You become it.

Heavy-laden with fruit
you approach the sacrificial vessel
and offer to life
your Self.

Cinders ebb
on coral-dripping stone
sagging embers grapple
fading dust
spasms groan in granite
bring forth rain.

DANCE II

Dawn,
in her bloody afterbirth
rains peace
upon a sodden
ground

Dawn: Mist Over Santa Cruz

This yeast that clouds and scars
and banters raindrops to be bars
slides within an open seam
and cracks the walls of village green
and stars so bright
and pewtered hovels craving light
and takes me
Home
to me
to Thee.

THE VISIT

Dancing tresses of evening
fondle memories,
and make of these meticulous musings
mystic paeans.

Silent Shades

A softer silence resounds
stirring chords of emptiness

muted pain ensues
trailing shafts of momentary bliss

a deeper silence pervades. . . .

*a dim whisper
echoes fitfully
beneath
an onrushing
stream.*

roots stalk fluid earth.

grace milks ether
from splintered stone.

a tattered flame
leaps into
oblivion
and dies.

wings pierce
naked air

thoughts float
safely
to higher ground.

a tremulous wave
weaves distances
through sordid currents.

gentle reeds
entwine perception
ground and molded
in endless shades.

victory spawns tentacles
that grip the knave
of hearts.

dreams spurn rushes
of tassled chimes.

incandescent waters
conjure up strife.

beacons nestle in private slumber.

buoys reach rafters
beyond repair.

battered sinews
thrill precariously.

time lapses
into unbridled cadence.

darkness throttles blinding night.

union portends
onlyness
without fear.

Sleep dear friend, Mother

Notes Towards An Escape From Death

Children: Sleep dear friend, Mother
your frail self
as suppliant as a tree
leafless and dry
has snuggled our conflicts and dreams
like the harsh red
of the acki
harbours life

Woman: But look at my arms
my scrawny tendrils
they beg the heavens for mercy
to make me stay here
dry as grandmother's
everwilling breasts
warm like new blood
painful as a dying rose.

Children: Ah, the night winks
to herald your coming. . . .
you were gone
but we are still here
searching in every friend
for you.
You are to us
a myth, a tale
of woe?
every falling star
treasures our wish
to know the truth.

Woman: Yes, the vagrancy
of a falling star
is the very essence

of truth
the journey is always
to another point
of infinity
Truth, in reality,
its fickle personification
dwells in man's heart
a garrulous visitor.
But please go away
it is not yet your time
for sin and pain.

Children: What separates them then?
the joy in sharing pain
is love expressed.

Woman: We pray and weep
feel the sting
of wind and rain
a flower appears
dies and fades away
leaving us
the tree and I
eternal worshippers
at the shrine of hope.

Children: But your pain
it is so quick
too cancerous
without your acceptance
can it never be escaped?

Woman: Leave life then and live
it is the only way
not to wilt and die
escape the burden of realising
give of your honesty
your uncalculated humanity
and love
it is your world

                of simple dreams
                that I most cherish
                but you must go now
                and play your children's games
                leave me,
                the carrier of death
                in my womb
                until you learn to understand
                the meaning of things.

Children: But it is not death
                you harbour there
                it is life
                the eternal vision
                of sunrise and a song
                hope for eyes that see
                and clothe themselves
                in unconscious darkness.

Woman: To live with that blindness
                is as dismal and deceptive
                as death
                open your eyes
                let the truth of light
                wring tears
                of sweat and blood
                from them
                feast them
                upon soft petals
                opening and falling
                unnoticed
                into the chasm of time.
                But, so long. . . .

Children: No, no
                speak on
                so that your words
                do not fall
                like Catholic veils
                over our heads

Woman: Search them then
and see what they mean
be patient my little ones
time changes the meaning
and even questions
the significance
of words
for music and love
rest best together
in silence
it is only then
we hear
a heart
beat.

Children: We hear your voice
echoing now from
a nearer distance
are you still here?
you tread away
so softly
in your Sunday best. . . .

Woman: See the blinkering stars
messages of things to come
they are eyes
sparkling like beverages
mocking as lovers' laughter
yet comforting
in this vastness
like a friend
but think always
as flowers dance
in the silence of the wind
the greater joy
is in the pain